Magic Harbours

Jamie Owen

MAGIC HARBOURS

Photography by Martin Cavaney

GOMER

First Impression/2004

hardback: ISBN 1 84323 338 X
softback: ISBN 1 84323 464 5

© text: Jamie Owen
© photographs: Martin Cavaney

Jamie Owen has asserted his right
under the Copyright, Designs and
Patents Act, 1988, to be identified
as Author of this Work.

Printed in Wales at
Gomer Press, Llandysul, Ceredigion

For my family and friends

contents

acknowledgements

So many people helped us on our journey
around Wales – my thanks to the people who live
and work in the harbours we visited; the RNLI,
the harbour masters and pilots. Thank you also
to all the following: the crew of *Mascotte* – Tony,
Will and Paul Winter, Mags and John Hart
– who made the voyage a joy; Martin Cavaney
for his wonderful photography; Sara Allen, Chris
Howells, Rob Finighan, Jon Rees, Mary Adams,
Ann Summerhayes, Dafydd Parry, Helen Callaghan,
Richard Longstaff and Richard Bartley who made
up the radio and television production team from
Aspect Television – at sea and on land; Dewi
Vaughan Owen for his legal help with copyrights;
The National Watersports Centre at Plas Menai
for their hospitality; Clare Hudson and Martyn
Ingram, who commissioned the project; my editors
Gail Morris Jones and Julie Barton, who turned a
blind eye to my long absences from the BBC; Elgan
Davies at the Welsh Books Council for the design;
Edward Parry for his proof reading; Mairwen Prys
Jones and the staff at Gomer Press.

preface

It didn't take long for me to answer the question
– 'Would you be interested in sailing around the
harbours of Wales in a century-old boat?' This is
the diary of that journey. It's not a history, geology
or geography of the harbours – they are better
undertaken by greater writers than me these are
simply the notes I kept at the end of each day's
sailing. We were blessed with beautiful weather in
one of the hottest summers for years.

It's a fascinating time to explore the harbours
of Wales. Many of them grew from the beginnings
of our industrialisation, with the exporting of our
wealth of stone, slate, coal and iron. The harbours
prospered as industry thrived, and then many of
them declined as the individual industries faded.

A new century has witnessed the tide of tourism
and leisure washing new wealth into our once
jaded seaside towns. Sleeping giants like Burry Port,
Swansea, Milford, Pembroke Dock and Fishguard
are busy building new marinas or waterside
homes and businesses. Derelict docksides, quiet
for decades, are noisy again with the sound of
construction. We've fallen in love once more with
living and working by the water, a new generation
looking to the harbours to provide a future – not
just a past. And this sense of renewal was a
constant companion on our voyage.

Sailing around Wales offers a journey of
extraordinary contrasts: one moment a coastline
of outstanding natural beauty then, around the
next headland, oil refineries or a steelworks. We
could have raced around the coast in a speedboat
in a matter of hours but, in a Bristol Channel
Pilot Cutter, the voyage took weeks. It gave us the
chance to watch the world from a distance, to pass
by slowly on the water, to look on and leave quietly
on the high tide.

There are fascinating and obvious places omitted
from this trip for which I make no apology – except
to say that our destinations were dictated by the
tide, time and wind.

Altogether we sailed about three hundred
miles, visited nineteen ports of call and no one
wanted to leave *Mascotte* at journey's end – that
alone is some achievement for a crew living in the
confined space of an old boat. If you're searching
for the urban buzz and the bright lights then you'll
be disappointed with a journey like ours, but if
it's splendid scenery, real life adventure and the
company of friends you're after, then there is no
finer way to spend a summer.

Jamie Owen

'OF ALL THE WOMEN in the ports around the world, Cardiff girls were the best – but then, I've gorra to say that, haven't I?' Harry 'Shipmate' Cooke has cycled to Cardiff Bay on his ancient bike to wish us well on our sail around Wales.

'Mind you, that Salvation Army girl in the Virgin Islands was something else,' he laughed, 'she kept her 'at on . . .'

I decline the offer of his yellowing list of addresses. We both agree that, by now, the girls whose names he has in his little black book, even if they are still alive, will no longer be in possession of their own teeth.

Harry first went to sea when he was fourteen, over seventy years ago; in his time he ran blockades during the Spanish Civil War, dodged German U-boats and shipped all manner of precious cargo. I know that if it weren't for his declining years, he'd love to be back on an old sailing boat leaving harbour on the morning tide.

Cardiff in Harry's heyday was a teeming port of crews and captains who'd sailed the globe. His sepia tales of drinking, fighting, girls and adventures are a world away from the sanitised harbour where we stand today, the smells and the stories having been cleared away for visitors. Harry says he misses the stink and the sound

'I was born and brought up in Cardiff, but I didn't understand the city properly until I sailed past Penarth Head and into the tea-coloured waters of Cardiff Bay.'

Gwyneth Lewis, *Cardiff Central*

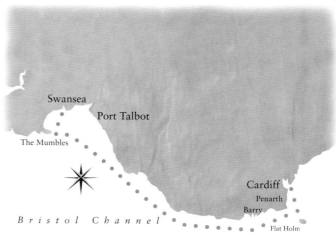

Cardiff Bay

of the old docks. When the steelworks were still firing, the evening goods train brought vats of white-hot dross from the furnaces to be tipped into the evening tide; then the sound of hot metal hitting cold salt water would race across the city.

Harry's mates – regulars at Solly Andrew's café, where they bought stewed tea, Fry's chocolate, Vimto and Navy Cut – are gone, long gone.

'You know, when old sailors die they become seagulls, shipmate?' said Harry, throwing more Mother's Pride into the water. 'These are me ol' mates.'

I don't know about his old mates but the gulls must think Christmas has come early.

I like the kind of people who hang around harbours: travellers arriving or departing on another voyage; dreamers – looking out to sea, planning an escape – who will never leave shore.

On a hot summer's day in August, it's slightly strange to be laden down with waterproofs and wet-weather gear. The one certainty of sailing round Wales in

Mascotte by the Norwegian Church

the summer is unpredictability. On the basis of past experience, we've all packed in the expectation of four seasons in as many days.

A century ago, Cardiff was one of the busiest commercial ports in the world. By the 1880s Cardiff had been transformed from one of the smallest towns in Wales to a port handling more coal than any other in the country. The international price of coal was struck at the exchange building in Mount Stuart Square, and it was there that the first ever million-pound deal was made. Today, where ships from around the globe would have once queued to tie up, holidaymakers sail around the bay in dinghies and speedboats. An assortment of expensive-looking yachts and their glamorous crews enjoy attention from the quayside.

Paul, Will and Tony Winter

I say goodbye to Harry and he wobbles off on his bike. 'Good luck, shipmate,' he shouts, looking like Captain Birdseye who has misplaced his boat.

At the end of the wooden jetty, *Mascotte* lies like a chapter from Harry's era, varnish and brass reflecting the afternoon sun. Walking down the wooden gangway I can't help feeling a sense of both excitement and trepidation; this will be a familiar journey around the harbours of Wales, some of which I know well, but in a hundred-year-old sailing boat, you expect the unexpected. For the coming weeks my life will be a series of destinations, the itinerary reading like a railway timetable without the times. High water and low water, the wind and the sea will determine the dates of our arrival and departure. If the sun continues to shine this will be a great journey; if, as on our last voyage together, rain and storm prevail, the coming days will be an endurance test.

Mascotte was built at the turn of the twentieth century as a functional working boat to deliver pilots to ships coming into harbour – so this trip is no jolly on a super-yacht. There are no luxuries on board, just uncomfortable bunks, wooden decks to sit on and ropes to rest against. The next weeks will throw my usual routine to the wind; we'll sail through the night, and days will begin in the dark. Yet for all that, this will be an adventure that will enchant us all.

Familiar welcomes on *Mascotte's* deck. Skipper Tony Winter is an entrepreneur who's spent a life in shipping – driving a desk, as he puts it, in the maritime industry. This boat is his weekend plaything. His son Will is back once more, having begun a new life with his wife since our last voyage together. Pilot John Hart and his wife Mags, our navigator, have also become good friends since our last adventure around the islands of Wales. We're to be joined on this trip by Tony's other son, Paul. Jon Rees our cameraman and Sara Allen the director team up again, this time with Helen Callaghan who's to make the radio series about our journey. We already know that we are too many to be comfortable on board. In dry weather it won't matter – we'll all be on deck; but sheltering from the elements down below, we'll have to get on well, very well.

The last supper

Below deck I try to make my luggage as small as possible in my bunk, but I've packed too much and there won't be room to lie flat tonight. Helen has brought twice as much luggage as the rest of us.

In the dying light of evening yellow flashes of sunlight catch the teak panelling of the companionway walls. Freshening up in the heads I remember that for the next two weeks a vital part of everyone's routine will be to pump out the toilet after using it.

Supper arrives: rice and meatballs, rice pudding and pears, washed down with a few glasses of wine. We all pause for a moment wondering where to sit down,

Shipping Forecast

CALM, FOG,
WEST, TWO OR THREE

and then it all comes flooding back from last time – you sit on the wooden deck. Helen can't believe she's sleeping in such a small bunk; she mistook it for a canvas shelf.

Moored opposite us is an ageing tug, *The Golden Cross*. While *Mascotte*'s new crew unpack, I walk on board to meet the tug's owners, Stuart and Susy White. Thirty years ago an ocean-going tug tied up along with dozens of other working boats wouldn't have looked out of the ordinary; now it attracts attention, it's out of place here. The vessel and her keepers have an intriguing history. *The Golden Cross* was the official escort to the Royal Yacht *Britannia*. Susy rescued the rotting hulk from a dock. In a previous life Susy was an actress and stunt co-ordinator in movies. She turned her back on the film industry for a life visiting the harbours of Europe in an old tug. At the end of the summer they'll follow in our wake and steam round Wales, bound for Liverpool. The galley is full of framed letters from Buckingham Palace, photos of their son in the Navy proudly displayed, and plaques from ports of call. They are on a mission to teach children about maritime history.

'It's strange to think that the grandparents of the South Wales schoolchildren who climb over this floating museum would all have known someone who worked in the docks, on the coal ships or in fishing, but within a couple of generations, we've lost touch with the sea,' Stuart says. He has a point. Cardiff Bay gives little away about its past – there's not much here to say that this was one of the greatest ports in the world. But Stuart and Susy tell everyone they meet.

We exchange goodnights and I turn in. Cardiff Bay's throbbing nightlife at the end of the pontoon will put paid to any hopes of a few hours' sleep on *Mascotte* before our departure at half-past four in the morning. I lie in my bunk and listen to a succession of terrible karaoke performances of 'Delilah'. Whoever said Wales was a land of song hadn't heard this lot.

'WHY, WHY, WHY, DEE – LI – LAH?'

It's boiling hot tonight – the middle of the heatwave. John Hart lumbers on deck to sleep; there's no breeze and the temperature below is soaring. John grapples with an inflatable airbed to make the planks more bearable. Since retirement from the pilot service he spends his life with Mags teaching sailing in Spain and delivering super-yachts to the super-rich around the world. He knows what he's let himself in for over the next few weeks.

'WHY, WHYYY, WHYYYY, DEE – LI – LAHHH?'

I spend hours trying to get comfortable on my bunk, ignoring another loud live crucifixion of 'Delilah' at the end of the jetty. In the end I give up and lie waiting for the early call.

Cardiff Bay's karaoke ends with a flourish that would have brought a tear to the eye of the deaf. In the silence that follows I can hear the restless movements of the crew, waiting another half-hour in their bunks for the off.

The Golden Cross, moored near *Mascotte*

The voyage begins,
past St David's Hotel

At half-past four, a dense sea-mist shrouds the bay; the place is deserted and still, save for a family of ducks marshalling their young across the water. We untie ropes on the pontoon, pass the St David's Hotel and make for the lock gate at Penarth, the two sentinels of a new chapter for Cardiff. Our horizons in every direction are new, built on the wastelands of the coal and steel dereliction of the 1980s. The old industries have gone and so have many of the people, moved out to make way for trendy waterside flats. This is still a housing and office development rather than a new community.

The Pierhead Building
The lock-gates of the barrage

In the darkness and mist, the barrage's flashing warning lights look like a crazed jukebox. Only milkmen and burglars see this hour of the day. The crew members go about their tasks in well-rehearsed silence. The last time we set off from here, twelve months ago, we turned back and were holed up in port for three days, beaten by the weather. Today I'm grateful even for the fog, since it means our journey has begun.

The lock-keepers blink out, bleary-eyed, at this 100-year-old sailing boat passing though their state-of-the-art barrage. I wonder what *Mascotte*'s original crew would have made of the damming of Cardiff Bay. Before its construction, the harbour experienced one of the world's greatest tidal ranges – up to 14 metres, drying out to mud flats – which inhibited the development of the docks.

Penarth pier prods the early mist, ghostly and deserted; only the seagulls are awake. We hoist the mainsail and set a course for Barry. Will and Paul rustle up breakfast of tinned kippers, eggs, tomatoes and steaming black coffee.

There is something timeless and romantic about leaving this harbour in heavy mist in a century-old boat. Sailors from across the world – India, China, Africa, Russia, France, Norway, Germany and Italy – have looked at these same hills, as they arrived and departed a hundred years ago. I thought again of Harry 'Shipmate' Cooke – he'd have loved this adventure.

Barry in the mist
Entrance to Port Talbot

John Hart takes up position in the bow to look out for buoys and listen for ships; visibility remains poor. We hoist a radar reflector to warn other vessels that we're somewhere out here in the fog. We stay well away from the main shipping lanes. Without GPS, the global positioning system that uses satellites to show you where you are, we wouldn't be making this trip – sailors of old would be safely tied up on shore.

We cling to the coast and nudge into Barry, past its lighthouse which guards the harbour. Over a century ago Rhondda's mine owners turned this small fishing village into the largest dock in the world. Then, after coal's demise, the banana boats from the West Indies kept the port alive until their vessels became too big to berth. Now chemicals, grain and timber from the Baltic unload here.

This morning at dawn, yachts, tugs and pilot boats are dotted around the water. Barry is a sleepy little place where no one sees *Mascotte* turn in full sail within the harbour walls.

Further along the coast, Rhoose, Breaksea, Nash Point, Porthcawl and Scar–water sands pass by in the cold small light of morning.

We make for Port Talbot – the fog is still low as tankers move slowly in and out of one of our busiest ports. This place sparks two reactions in the heart of South Walians: dismay at the sight of one of the most polluted towns in the country and

Port Talbot: fishing boats, ancient and modern

gratitude that – in a community that has lost much of its heavy manufacturing industry – it's still there. Ships have been sailing up to this shore for two thousand years: the Romans came first, then Celtic monks built churches in the now forgotten peace of Margam and Baglan. After a morning of ghostly emptiness on the water, the silent exit of a tanker gives all of us a start.

The entrance to Port Talbot is 50 feet wide, and its harbour has the deepest berthing facilities in the Severn Estuary area. The local RNLI crew head towards us in their inflatable rib – they're on an early training exercise. They've never seen anything like *Mascotte* in Port Talbot before, and as they speed away you realise how much a hundred years of innovation has changed the way we travel: their boat would cover the whole of the Welsh coast in hours, but it will take us days and days. As a child of the motor age I suddenly feel impatient with our slow progress in the breeze; it'll take some time to forget a life lived at a faster pace.

A few miles and a couple of hours along the coast, Mumbles is celebrating

Mumbles Sea Festival

– it's the Sea Festival and you can hear the music across the water. The fog has lifted and we come towards Mumbles Pier – a little too close for the liking of the assembled fishermen. When they know their lines are about to be cut they respond in a way that can only be described as 'the Swansea greeting', complete with ancient words and gestures. As we drop anchor I can see giant pirates on land and hear sea shanties in the distance. Three of us hoist *Mascotte*'s punt over the side and pull up its little sail. There's barely enough wind to blow the small boat to the shore on this blistering day.

Mumbles is crowded with people enjoying the festival – jugglers, mime artists, rescue-dogs, lifeboat displays, speedboats, burger-bars, screaming children and scowling parents. We are all in shock that the sun is out this summer – it has caught us unawares. At the ice cream parlour on the seafront dozens of families watch the world and each other go by. eyes peer out between huge peach melbas and chocolate sundaes. This is Britain by the sea in August; there is no chic fashion parade here, no continental promenade of the svelte and the starved. Here T-shirts too small for big bellies barely cover white, pink and red flesh; sunburnt skin and last year's shorts are the order of the day. Dogs fight in the heat, distracted only

Film crew at the lifeboat station

Swansea Marina

by the feast of chips and burgers. A queue of traffic begins a symphony of discord; at weekends, rush-hour gridlock moves to the beach.

Back on the water, there's a mad dash for the lock at Swansea marina. After the neap tides there's just enough water for *Mascotte* over the Towy lock. The lock-keepers issue a tired warning over the PA speakers to the kids jumping into the dark water. We're directed to our berth on the Museum pontoon.

A vision in checks and white walks along the harbour wall. Chef Chris Keenan is the new man at the five-star Morgan's hotel in Swansea. As a favour, he's offered to come and cook for us on his night off. Laden with fish and herbs he jumps onto the deck and disappears below to find the galley. Morgan's maestro turns pale when shown the paraffin cooker in the three-foot-square galley. He's used to greater things, but is kind enough not to say so. On deck the fumes from paraffin and meths are soon replaced by enticing wafts from warming food. Chris has spent the morning at Swansea market, a temple of local vegetables, meat, poultry and fish to which people come from miles around to buy the laverbread and cockles.

The chef's splendid fish with peppers is almost wasted on a tired crew who crave their bunks, but empty plates soon display our gratitude. Chris may not have cooked on two rings on a paraffin stove before, but you'd never have guessed it. His summer will be spent persuading the guests at the hotel to try unfamiliar dishes of Welsh food and weaning them off the international fare offered in every hotel around the world. He wishes us well on our voyage and in a flash of white disappears with his saucepans.

On deck after a long day another bottle of wine is opened. I stretch out and smile at the thought of life at sea for the next few weeks and no office grind. Will and Paul have left behind a pregnant wife and a new mother respectively. Their evening ritual revolves around hushed mobile-phone calls, both assuring their Mrs Winters that this is not a drunken jolly but hard work. They are here to help their father pilot this old boat round Wales, but it's clear that their loyalties have been stretched.

I settle down for an hour with my sailing manual. I'm going to be examined at the end of this voyage for my Competent Crew Certificate, but learning on *Mascotte* is like taking driving lessons in a vintage car. She's a century old and, my incompetence aside, she won't be the easiest vessel to learn on. Whenever skipper Tony shouts an instruction about the port beam, starboard quarter, the bow or the stern, or

Chef Chris Keenan

motions to the sails and barks an order about the tack, luff or clew, I hestitate, as if translating from a foreign language, before scurrying off – usually in the wrong direction.

Cameraman Jon Rees goes for a walk around the marina. After the terrible karaoke in Cardiff Bay last night, we're all looking forward to some undisturbed sleep. Jon returns, and just as we head for bed, we realise we've tied up in earshot of the marina's gay bar, where slow ballads like 'Stand By Your Man' start to be walloped out at top volume. Everyone is so exhausted that it's only a matter of minutes before tiredness overwhelms us.

Sunset in Swansea

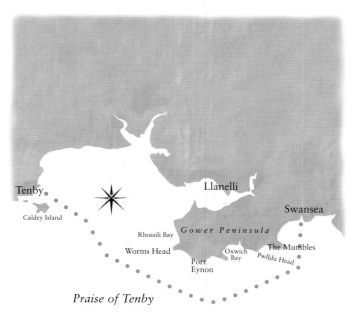

Praise of Tenby

There is a fine fortress on the height,
Its feasting lavish, its revelry loud,
Lovely about it, that camp of heroes,
Is the wandering spray, long are its wings.'

Welsh poem, Anonymous, c. 875

THUNDER AND LIGHTNING wakes us at 7am. It's been swelteringly hot all week and we're hoping the electric storm will clear the air. We're spending the rest of the day in Swansea before heading for Tenby tonight. Breakfast of tea and toast then off to meet Andrew Lamnea of Trinity House, which looks after navigation buoys and lighthouses.

Freight trains trundle lethargically through the docks. This is the gritty bit of Swansea's maritime quarter, a world away from the swanky yachts and the marina apartments.

Trinity House looks like a giant toy-shop of swollen magic mushrooms. Fifteen-foot-high buoys in red, green, yellow and black lie across the yard, waiting for a new coat of paint and a high tide to sweep them back into the water. Most have names painted on their sides: *BRIGHTON PIER WEST, BIDEFORD BAR, PRINCE IVANHOE, BOLIVAR, MOSTYN, ZEALANDIA* and *MORTE STONE*. Each buoy has a unique number of light

Fishermen
cast off

Buoys at Trinity House

flashes, which would once have been powered by oil, but now solar panels fire up the warning beacons. Andrew shows me into an old stone building where tired buoys are stripped, blasted, welded and repainted. Here lamps are lovingly repaired and beacons refitted, all fixed by craftsmen who've done the job for decades.

One of the fitters says this work is like waving off your kids and then seeing them return once in a while for some tender loving care. It is more than a labour of love, though: ships, passengers and crews the length of Britain depend on what's being done here. The men at Trinity House in Swansea are responsible for all the pilotage on the west coast of Britain – all the buoys, navigation beacons and lighthouses. Countless ships pass through these waters and many of those aboard them never know how obliged they are to these men.

Andrew's ancestors were Greek sailors who fell in love with Swansea and never left. He worked in Swansea docks when the port was still

Andrew Lamnea

Helwick lightship

buzzing with commercial traffic. That's all but gone now, but the redevelopment of the old docks suggests that maybe Swansea's bad times are in the past. The next big business is leisure and the city's plan is for more marina development, waterside apartments and cashing in on our renewed love affair with the sea.

Back beside *Mascotte*, in the marina, the keeper of the lightship *Helwick* is polishing his pride and joy. Tied to the museum quay, the *Helwick* was built in the 1930s and was anchored on Helwick Sands outside Swansea to warn mariners of impending grounding. She has no engine and was towed to her location and staffed by lightkeepers. The job's done by an unmanned lightbuoy these days. The men of the *Helwick* are gone the way of the lighthouse keepers – into the history books.

Time to go – we untie our ropes and pass through the lock gates. The next shift of kids jump off the quayside and annoy the lock-keepers.

Swansea Bay has a handful of fishing boats, yachts and jet skis enjoying the evening sunshine. I sit on the ropes in the bow and look out for lobster pots as we pick our way out of the channel. All sails aloft: mainsail, top sail and balloon jib. We hug the coast and make for Tenby – it'll take us some six hours. There's a wonderful sunset tonight, with ten miles visibility. Through binoculars I can see Milford Haven's roaring chimneys and Caldey Island. On a beam reach this is going to be a wonderful sail in fresh winds.

On the starboard side, The Mumbles, Bracelet Bay, Oxwich, Helwick and Worm's Head are all left behind.

Our paraffin cooker has given up the ghost after the exertions of the five-star chef, Chris Keenan. Supper tonight will be cold: lettuce, tomatoes, potato salad, bread, apples, bananas and beer. We'll get the cooker fixed in Milford in a couple of days.

Gower's coast disappears into the night and Pembrokeshire lies before us. Tonight it's cooler, like a proper Welsh August. T-shirts get covered up with fleeces and pullovers as evening draws in.

In the last light of the evening Cefn Sidan Sands slip by, behind them Laugharne and Pendine Sands. The chart shows an area marked 'Trawler's Dread' in the middle of Carmarthen Bay, a reminder of its treacherous sandbars and infamous wrecks. We plot a course for Monkstone Point on the Pembrokeshire coast.

Tenby's chart displays a history of sailing that is centuries old: Bowman's Point looks out over Tenby Roads, Woolhouse rocks, Man-of-War Roads, and Jones Bay. The names tell of a more colourful age.

We arrive outside Tenby harbour at eleven and St Mary's spire looks spectacular from the water. In the darkness we move gingerly up and down the bouys looking for the RNLI mooring, which they've kindly given us permission to use overnight. The harbour is strewn with buoys and lobster pots and, in the dark, finding one

Shipping Forecast

CALM, NORTH-WEST,
FOUR OR FIVE

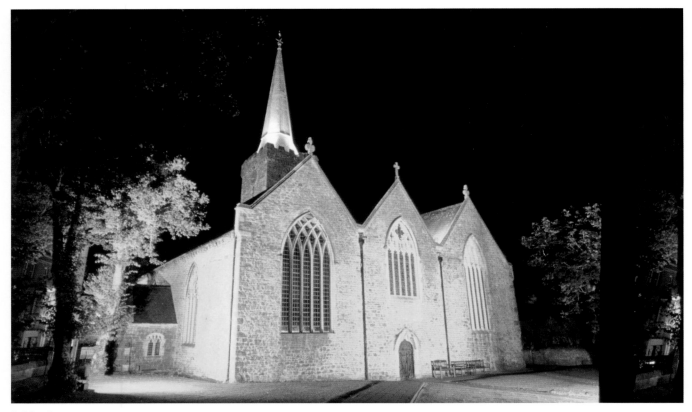

St Mary's

mooring among a hundred is no easy task. Skipper Tony is anxious that we'll snag the propeller, there's so little water beneath the keel. John Hart flashes a beam to wash the black water with light. *Mascotte* is too heavy to tie up to anything other than the lifeboat mooring.

Dropping anchor where we are would mean snagged chains and ropes and anchor watch all night for the crew. We need to find that mooring. John calls Tenby's RNLI coxswain who talks us into position by mobile phone. Finally, an hour after arriving, we pull the buoy aboard and tie up. There's about six feet of water beneath the keel and the tide is going out. Tony discovers we've snagged a lobster pot on the way in.

Tenby harbour
Tenby lifeboat house

Shipping Forecast

CALM, WEST,
TWO OR THREE

Tenby harbour at evening

Queue for the boat to Caldey Island
Museum curator, John Beynon

For all its difficulties this is one of the most beautiful places we will sail to. The castle, small harbour and the grand houses above it frame a perfect setting for a nightcap before sleep. All night we will be gently rocked by the swell.

At half-past seven in the morning, we all head for shore in the punt, pushing through the harbour water jumping with fat mullet. Tenby's asleep. The tourists and townsfolk are tucked up in the yellow, blue, pink and cream houses that line the clifftop. Dozens of local boats hug the harbour wall, empty for another half an hour, and then the place comes to life. Fishermen and boat crews queue at a stall for their bacon rolls and black tea before casting off and landing mackerel – or day trippers, or both.

Coxswain Alan Thomas brings the Caldey Island boat alongside the wall. Today the vessel is carrying the island's cattle to market on the mainland. I thank him for his help with the mooring last night. Generously he says arriving in Tenby by night isn't easy in a big boat, even for a local skipper.

Like a scene from *Under Milk Wood*, the regular cast of Tenby harbour begin to arrive, accompanied by the changing characters of holidaymakers and day trippers already filling the town beach.

John Beynon is the museum's curator. We sit on the town wall and ponder the changing fortunes of the town. The museum displays some wonderful old photographs of Victorian bathing machines – enclosed wooden carts that were led

Tenby Castle

by horses a little way into the sea to allow bathers to swim fully clad away from the prying eyes of the townspeople. A few yards from us today sun-worshippers stripping off for a day's tanning leave little to the imagination.

As curator of the Castle Museum, John has a particular fondness for the castle itself. Despite being badly damaged during the Civil War, one imposing tower of the 13th-century castle still stands on the rocky headland. An even earlier earthwork castle stood here; as early as 1153 it was captured by the Welsh and Llywelyn, last Prince of Wales, sacked the town during his campaign of 1260.

One of the other buildings in Tenby which tourists visit in growing numbers is the Tudor Merchant's House, now owned by the National Trust. Tucked in

Clem and Edna Jenkins, my grandparents
Tudor Merchant's House

between other buildings on narrow Quay Hill, the Merchant's House gives a good idea of town life in fifteenth-century Wales. Outside is a small herb garden of the kind a Tudor family would have kept.

In the heat of midday I thought for a moment I saw my grandmother. She is long, long gone, but my memories of Tenby are of visiting with my grandparents. From the age of five or six, for part of the summer holidays, I would stay with them at their cottage in Moreton, Saundersfoot. They were Victorians, in the sense that they were brought up by Victorian parents themselves and that informed their own behaviour. Little boys were to be seen and not heard. They took a dim view of 1970s Tenby, which they saw as sliding down market into low-rent hotels and sleazy summers. This was a time when the Costas were on the rise and the only refuge for the British seaside holiday-resorts was in cost-cutting kiss-me-quick vacations.

Despite the one-way signs and double yellow lines, my grandparents continued to drive around Tenby as they had done for forty years, stopping outside every shop, conducting their business and then moving on. Every Saturday, my grandfather – a man of few words – would be left in the car with me, until motioned to come and carry fruit, groceries or meat into the boot of their black Morris Minor. Or on other weekends, if their hens laid well, eggs would be carried to sell in the Star shop in the square.

For decades, there was no deviation in their routine. The weekly trip seemed to take the same amount of preparation as loading elephants for a journey across India. The black car was washed and polished in the morning. Then it was time to wash and change. It was best clothes on, which meant that even in a steaming July, Grampa wore his three-piece tweed suit and a flat cap and Gran a substantial outfit of heavy cloth and a large hat. It was important to dress well;

Tenby harbour-front
The Morris Minor and family

Tenby town houses

it gave a good impression, she said. Three wicker shopping baskets were loaded into the back of the Morris – plastic bags were never used.

In his retirement my Grandfather reasoned that there were few pressing engagements in his diary and his motoring was conducted at speeds no faster than forty miles an hour. In winter, the road from Saundersfoot to Tenby was empty most afternoons, but in the summer holidays, when Birmingham and Manchester decamped en masse to Pembrokeshire, the road was packed. Grampa rarely looked in his rear view mirror so I put myself in charge of watching what was behind. It was usually Mr and Mrs Psychopath from Solihull shaking their fists after we'd nonchalantly pulled out in front of them and slowed their sprint to the caravan. Apart from Grampa's unique driving technique, there was the Morris's own arthritic contribution to manoeuvres. The sound of engine and exhaust was like a three-minute warning to oncoming motorists and pedestrians. The car had no flashing indicators, just little orange, semaphore signals that stuck out of the side. So our entrance into Tenby was always at the head of a long, slow snake of traffic, no doubt trailing back hundreds of miles to the Midlands, but the orchestra of complaining car horns behind went unnoticed in the front seat of the Morris.

Our first stop was always Smith's on the seafront, to buy *Country Life* and *Woman's Weekly*, then to the fruit and vegetable shop opposite. Gran had never worked and had no conception of other people's time; she always asked after the shop owner's health and, although she'd known some of them for four decades, they still all called her Mrs Jenkins. Gran's big day out was Saturday shopping in Tenby and she enjoyed taking her time. It was a ceremony, a tradition; if shopkeepers replied that they were under the weather or had suffered some family trouble or were on the edge of the abyss, Gran would unfailingly offer comprehensive advice on what course of action to take next, no matter how long the queue of waiting shoppers. It was all part of her weekly missionary work.

After stocking up with groceries in the Star shop it was on to the butcher and T. P. Hughes opposite. TP's is Tenby's department store where, a couple of years later, the small Owen brothers had a splendid fight in one of the windows, knocking down one of the mannequins. Whilst my grandmother shopped and talked at length, my grandfather would be boiling outside in his suit in the black Morris.

Even as a small boy I knew what a double yellow line, a one-way system, and a traffic warden signified, and I sat back on the red leatherette seats waiting for the worst. My grandparents reasoned that all the signs were for the tourists and not the locals. The traffic warden was invariably dismissed with routine disdain by my grandmother, resplendent in a Saturday hat, bedecked with a variety of dead feathered livestock.

My grandparents never went to a supermarket, they spoke to everyone they met and the whole adventure took the best part of half a day. But then, no one was counting the hours. It seems like yesterday.

By the time we return to *Mascotte* the tide has gone out and the tender is on the sand. Dinghies, speedboats, fishing vessels, pleasure boats are all left high and dry, clinging to ropes tied to ancient stones. On the beach, families nestle behind windbreaks, children play football, teenagers pull sailing club boats onto their trolleys.

Looking on are grey-haired day trippers, just off a coach, sitting on the benches on the clifftop. The descent to the sands and the pull back up the steep steps would be too much for them: better to sit and stare at the ships sailing by.

Mascotte moored off Monkstone Point

Tide on the turn

T E N B Y   T O   M I L F O R D

A WONDERFUL AFTERNOON'S SAILING in bright sunshine from Tenby to Milford, past Penally, Caldey Island, Priest's Nose, Manorbier Castle, Swanlake Bay, Freshwater East, Barafundle and Broadhaven. Near St Govan's Head the range boat from Castlemartin comes alongside and orders us to change course – they send us two miles off shore to avoid the firing practice from the land. I've never been this close to the coastline here; the sandstone and limestone Stack Rocks are spectacular. There are no yachts here, no other craft in sight. If this were the south coast of England, the water would be heaving with sailing boats. Not that I wish for that, but the Essex boys, Tony, Will and Paul, are silent witnesses to the beauty of this stretch of coast and mystified as to why we don't make more of our extraordinary asset.

St Govan's Head and its tiny chapel pass slowly by. Govan was a hermit who devoted himself to a life of prayer, choosing a spectacular setting halfway down this cliffside for his cell. But he was also concerned for the safety of mariners and legend has it that he rang a bell to warn ships of the treacherous rocks near the headland, and often helped shipwrecked sailors to safety. Pirates and wreckers were none too pleased with his interference, and plotted to murder him. The saintly Govan fled and hid in a crevice in the rocks.

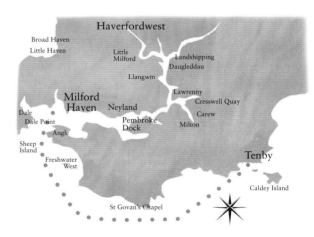

'Say…how far it is
To this same blessed Milford: and,
        by the way,
Tell me how Wales was made so happy as
T'inherit such a haven'
Cymbeline Act III, Scene ii,
William Shakespeare

St Govan's chapel

Sailing past Manorbier cliffs

Bathers at Manorbier

There's a steady breeze and soon Saddle Head, Moody Nose and Bullslaughter Bay disappear behind us. We are heading for Freshwater West beach to look at the seaweed hut where laverbread was processed a century ago. Once there were a dozen huts here, reminders of a time when we ate everything the seaside had to offer; now there's just one left. Up-market restaurants make a big thing of dishes with laverbread now, but it has disappeared from most of our plates, a victim of the supermarket culture. Chef Chris Keenan told us he offers laverbread in his restaurant in Swansea – a food that was once commonplace has become a delicacy within a generation.

On the cliff before Freshwater are the outlines of the tank decoys and above them sporadic puffs of white smoke from the artillery exercises on the military training range. It's as well we changed course.

Lunch consists of cold pilchards, bread and salad, whilst Will hooks a few mackerel on the line off the stern; arrangements are in place for a new cooker to be delivered at Milford tomorrow.

Milford Haven's refinery chimneys puncture the sky, while Monk Rock, Parsonsquarry Bay, Sheep Island, Rat Island and Thorn Island all lie ahead of us. West Angle Beach is packed with families lying in the sun.

At four o'clock, off Freshwater West, with the Castlemartin peninsula fading behind us, Dale and Angle come into view on either side of the estuary, and we enter Milford Haven. The frantic concentration in this narrow funnel of water of ferries, tankers, tugs, speedboats and fishermen is something of a shock after the solitude of the day's sail in open sea.

Nelson described Milford as one of the greatest harbours in the world and Daniel Defoe was similarly generous, calling it one of the best inlets in Britain. George Owen (no relation), writing in the sixteenth century, said it was 'a large and spacious harbour sufficient to receive the greatest vessel of whatsoever burden that saileth on the seas.'

The defensive forts built in Napoleonic times must have turned this stretch of river into a snipers' alley that would give an enemy vessel entering the Haven no chance at all. As it happened, the enemy never came, at least not here.

In the nineteenth century, pioneering American Quaker whalers sailed into Milford with whale oil to be used to light up London. The town of Milford was built around a grid system, like Pembroke Dock on the other side of the river, and its development as a town was eclipsed by Pembroke Dock's rise. Nonetheless, Milford became an important fishing port, reaching its height in the 1920s when thousands were employed in the industry. In the post-war years, fishing declined but then came the oil industry boom, particularly following the Suez crisis. The landscape today on both sides of the river is dominated by massive refinery chimneys and jetties.

St Govan's chapel
Stack Rock fort

An hour after entering the harbour, in little wind, we make it through the lock at Milford and tie up beside the fish market. We've an early start tomorrow, and don't want to have to travel too far from our bunks.

Trawler skipper Coolsaet Dirk
Mascotte arriving at Milford

Shipping Forecast

NORTH-WEST, THREE

Wednesday 0600 Milford Docks

Bleary-eyed, we prepare ourselves for the jaunt to the electronic fish market. A trawler arriving from the Bristol channel, *Ster Der Zee*, makes its way through the lock gate and minutes later ties up alongside us. In a well-rehearsed routine, an articulated truck parks up, ready to load fish bound for Belgium. The ship's skipper, Coolsaet Dirk, has been in the business for 23 years and looks how a trawler skipper should look: bearded and menacing. On his first trips to Wales, he tells us, Milford had dozens of trawlers but now there are only a handful. On this trip he's been at sea for thirteen days and they've caught five tons of fish. His wife, a local woman, meets him on the quay.

The trawlers are Anglo-Spanish, and to comply with EU law a portion of the catch must be landed and sold here. The skipper launches into a tirade over fishing quotas and says he doesn't want his kids to go to sea, because the glory days are over. I ask him for his solution to the crisis in fish stocks. 'Smaller boats and an end to the factory ships,' he suggests. Dirk says his crew are leaving to work on

Entering the harbour

the dredging boats back home because it's more lucrative. None of them goes to the electronic auction – they don't need to ask the market prices for their catch.

A stone's throw from the trawler, the fishmarket is a soulless affair. It's a large modern barn in which buyers sit on plastic chairs at computer desks, drowsy at their terminals but with one eye on a projection on the wall of shifting prices and ships. Around Europe, buyers log on to a dutch auction and press Return on their keyboards when they like the price. The whole process is conducted in silence. I'd expected sellers shouting prices and throwing cod. The auctioneer,

Hefyn Williams, says prices are low because of the hot weather. Fish doesn't travel or keep well in warm temperatures. On the other side of the barn are the boxes of fish I'd expected to see, with bright labels indicating their species and the trawler's name.

Across the way from here, opening early, is the town's maritime museum. Its photographs from seventy years ago show how the harbour was lined with trawlers from end to end. It all makes for a rather poignant morning.

Sitting on the quayside looking across Milford, I have a view which takes in the major themes of Wales's maritime story, or at least, the latest chapter in that story. On one side of the docks are the fishing trawlers, with their crews mending their nets and painting over rusty metal in blue, black and yellow; on the other side is the new marina, full of expensive yachts. Milford is nearly thriving again, and pleasure not work, is one of the new businesses.

The other big business here is oil, turning thick crude black stuff into fuel for cars, trucks and planes. The nerve centre of Milford Haven Port Authority looks like air traffic control – full of radar screens – and its job is just as indispensible. The oil

Milford marina

tankers coming in and out of here every hour are difficult to manoeuvre and almost impossible to stop. This office has the impossible task of balancing the industrial development of the port with the environmental conservation of the waterway. Talk this morning is of the missing swimmer who disappeared last night, trying to cross Milford Haven after a good night in a bar. An all-night search found their man safely asleep all along, albeit in somebody else's bed.

At the end of the Port Authority's jetty are a couple of pilot boats, tied up ready for work. These are the modern equivilent of *Mascotte*. Tony, Will and

Paul would have liked to have seen these but cooker duties detain them. This is the business end of bringing huge boats safely to harbour. It's as simple and terrifying as it ever was. A small boat delivers an experienced local man who knows the waters, on board a huge ship. He leaps daringly across the water, climbs a rope ladder and then, with a skilled and experienced hand, brings the vessel safely to her berth.

On board the pilot boat we meet the skipper, then we're off immediately to collect a pilot from aboard a supertanker docking at the jetty nearby. Within yards of this massive concentration of heavy industry flutter the triangles of twenty yachts in reds, whites and blues on a day's sail. This waterway is an odd mix of business and pleasure.

The pilot, Captain Andy Darlington, is a modest man just doing his job, jumping on and off ships at sea, but both crew and cargo depend on his skill for safe passage. We have a brief chat before the VHF radio barks instructions for the next ship awaiting pilotage.

Fishing boat returning
Harbour tug
Pilot, Andy Darlington

Supertanker entering Milford

Dropping the pilot onto the supertanker looks terrifying even on a calm day. The skipper manages a controlled collision to bring pilot boat and tanker together – it is perhaps one of the few times ships collide intentionally. The sheer size of the tanker viewed from a small boat is daunting. The pilots' and the Port Authority's work is like choreographing dinosaurs. The tanker crew, men with hard hats, wave down at us. No doubt they are frequent visitors to these waters yet they hardly step ashore, such is the life of an international seaman. They seem genuinely pleased to have reached land after weeks on the ocean, as if, despite global positioning systems, radar and all the technology modern shipping has at its disposal, they are still grateful for safe deliverance. As with all the sailors I meet, I can't help wondering how much they really see of their destinations; perhaps it's the lure of the sea that holds the fascination, not exploring foreign countries.

The tanker crew throw a series of ropes to the nearby tug. This is a new development in procedure since the *Sea Empress* oil tanker disaster here; all vessels are now accompanied into port with a line attached to a tug, so in the event of steering failure or loss of power, help is already in place.

On our return into Milford, porpoises play off the bow but, infuriatingly, whenever our camera is pointed at them, they'll switch to another quarter of the boat. Cameraman Jon Rees and director Sara Allen are convinced the actors' union EQUITY must have a porpoises' branch, but these animals have no contract. Jon and Sara begin pleading with the creatures to appear in the programme – much to the amusement of the pilot boat crew. Eventually the porpoises oblige and their show is delightful.

Tea is brewed and mugs handed round; this has been a fascinating day. Tony and John Hart have a stock of tales about the courage of the men of the pilot boats – John himself was a pilot. But to see them in action, taking that leap of faith across the water, is enthralling. Milford is the busiest port we've been to and to watch a working harbour at close quarters in the company of such talented and self-effacing people has been time well spent.

Gelliswick Bay

Milford welcomes the *Astor*

Signal flags

The boat drops us off at the jetty and turns to service another vessel.

At midday a German liner, *Astor*, starts delivering her passengers ashore by tender at Milford. Beyond a large white marquee, full of tourist information and a craft stand, coaches wait, marked 'St David's Cathedral' and 'Tenby'. This is Milford Haven's newest cargo. For a generation that grew up with the jet, aspiring to escape to the sun, Milford would not have been high on a list of must-see destinations; but in a time of terrorism and frequent vacations, the idea of sailing around Britain, particularly during a warm summer like this, is not unattractive. Milford Haven is the obvious place to anchor a massive cruise ship since there are few other locations on this stretch of water which could accommodate it. And Tenby, the National Botanic Garden in Carmarthenshire, and St David's Cathedral are as beautiful as any far-flung location. Pembrokeshire's finest have arrived in droves to see this huge white ship in the waterway – many are glad that their town is once again back on the map. An old guy smiles as he says, 'The last time this many Germans were in Pembrokeshire was with the Luftwaffe.'

On the bridge of *Astor*

The ship's lifeboat delivers its first shuttle of thirty tourists to the old mackerel stages and offers us a lift to the vessel. With murmured agreement not to mention the war, we jump aboard *Astor*. Her crew is mostly Russian, 'Vladimir' and 'Yuri' neatly typed on their name-badges. The officers are sleeping, because the ship travels by night and anchors by day. Today's tour is marked up in the central enquiries area as 'Milford Haven, England'. The passengers have less than a day in Milford Haven, England before travelling to Ireland at 18.00 tonight; this really is Britain in a hurry. As is the way of cruise ships, those who remain on board are too wobbly to cope with the tenders to shore, just content to watch the world go by from the safety of the ship.

Astor left Bremerhaven four days ago for Plymouth on a 14-day voyage, taking in Milford Haven, Cork, Dublin, Oban, Stornoway, Inverness, Edinburgh and London before returning home.

Posters on the ship's gangways advertise 'Merry old England, Big Ben, *der* Buckingham Palace, *der* Tower, Piccadilly Circus *und viele wahrhaft konigliche Bauwerke*' illustrated with a Beefeater and a horned Highland steer.

The passengers' daily diary pinned up on notice boards gives a useful insight into why the trains always run on time back home. At 7am, *Guten Morgen!* Corina, a splendid blonde, beams from the wall offering *der Morgenwecker zum Wachwerden am Mikrofon auf Kanal 11hrs Bordradios.* No sooner are Corina's early exertions over than at 8am *Fit in den Tag* on the sportdeck with . . . Corina. Followed half an hour later by *Walking in den Morgen* with Henk, wearing full traditional Bavarian costume. At 9am, it's time for a little *Bauch-Beine-Po-Gymnastik* with the generously built Madeleine. From her photo I think it's safe to assume she simply gives orders rather than engaging in too much *gymnastik*. Oberstewardess Marita Ruff offers a well-earned cake in the Ubersee Club at 10.30 by which time the splendid Corina and Henk join forces for Volleyball. No wonder the Germans are throwing themselves into the tenders for St Davids: they must be knackered.

Back on shore a few hours later, the tourists have returned from their visits, and the Haverfordwest Male Voice Choir speed the passengers' departure. Milford's grandees hope this trip will mean many happy returns; four hundred wealthy people buying tours and teas is not to be sniffed at. One of those summer sea mists rolls in and envelops the ship for a few minutes and then lifts as quickly as it arrived. The cruise passengers must think this is the last in an impressive list of local features.

Astor's crew start busying themselves on deck for departure for Ireland. Passengers have *Broadway Melodien* to look forward to tonight, *Eine Reise in die Welt der Musicals. Kersten Wiecha, zu Gast: Dance Magic* to keep them going across St George's Channel. As on all good ships the day ends on the *Astor* at 23.00 with Happy Hour in *der Hanse Bar!* Bon Voyage.

Back in the docks, a small van pulls up alongside *Mascotte*, and a man with a cooker appears. Tony, Will and Paul spend ages manhandling it into the galley, itself not much bigger than the cooker. Director Sara Allen, Cameraman Jon Rees and I set off on a brief mission to Milford's shops – it's John Hart's birthday tomorrow and we have to find a cake and some champagne for a secret celebration at sea. An hour later, every store scoured, we return looking shifty with parcels.

On the quayside, Gordon Parry, a family friend, rolls up to wish us well. He grew up around here and remembers a harbour full of fishing boats in his childhood. Gordon once stood for Parliament in Pembrokeshire and my father helped him with his campaign. I remember walking around housing estates delivering Gordon's election literature. My brother Huw and I could only just reach the door bells. We would tap the doors on one side of the street while Dad did the other. I've no idea if the voters thought we were two sweet little boys or that their prospective MP was a promoter of child labour!

It's time to leave. On the way out of Milford a tall, distinguished-looking man with white hair stands at the edge of the lock looking down. He smiles. I smile back and know his face is familiar. I walk to the bow and rack my brains, run back to the stern and shout to him, 'Denis Cole, Pennar School?' He taught me 25 years ago across the water from here. In art lessons, he made his small charges turn their desks away from the blackboard and towards the window. My art disappointed him, but the view of the ships arriving and departing inspires me to this day. I've a lot to thank him for but we grab only a few crowded seconds, passing each other in the lock gate.

We head up the river Cleddau. Over the water is Hobbs point, Pembroke Dock, which is where we used to catch the ferry when I was little, before the bridge was built. My parents took us to the nearby hill after school one day to see where the box girder

The late Lord Parry of Neyland
Memorial to sailors lost at sea, Milford

bridge had fallen into the water in mid-build. The bridge was rebuilt succesfully, of course, but ever since, West Walians have always been slightly sceptical about people with big plans.

Passing Pembroke Dock
Dad, Huw, Richard and me

This is where I grew up, so I've spent my life leaving Pembroke Dock one way or another. My Dad was born and brought up here; he loved the town with a passion that I never understood. In my childhood it felt like a place forgotten and left behind in the slipstream of history; unemployment and poverty were never far away. Although we had a privileged upbringing, Dad's solicitor's practice and Mum's work as health visitor highlighted the difficulties this community faced. People dealt an unlucky hand were regular visitors to our house. It was a community that waited in suspense for a big jobs announcement that would be salvation for an economy far from the wealthy cities. I remember feeling despair when, years later, I had to read the news on television of the loss of the much-heralded 1000-jobs call centre in the town. I knew how much it would hurt this small community. Big idea, badly thought out and short-lived.

To me, as a youngster, the old home town seemed a dump best escaped from as soon as possible for the bright lights of anywhere else. Visits home were always filled with Dad's hope for the declining town. After years working in London and then Cardiff I still didn't understand his deep affection for Pembroke Dock. The town's heyday had passed generations before, when PD, as it is affectionately known, was a Royal Dockyard. After that closed in 1926 the town would never again enjoy the prosperity that it had known then.

Dad and his brothers lived on the shore's edge in Water Street, a childhood spent swimming, messing about in boats and on the beach. In an age before the oil industry's chimneys, the estuary must have been idyllic. The three brothers were split up by the outbreak of war in 1939; they all joined up and were posted around the world when they were no more than teenagers. Dad's letters home from India, Hong Kong and Burma over seven years tell the story of a boy, like millions of others, pulled from adolescence and thrust into a foreign and violent world. For him it was an adventure that no other could ever surpass. And far from home, he viewed the family, friends and the town he'd left behind through a romantic perspective.

Decades later Dad would spend hours researching the personal stories of the people in the town during the time he was away; tales of evacuees, the bombings, the postings and school pals who would never return. After the war, apart from the time when he trained for law, he would only reluctantly leave Pembroke Dock. It was as though he spent the rest of his life trying to wrest back the years taken away.

Pembroke Dock Guntower Museum

The Cleddau Bridge

When my father died a few years ago I walked into St John's church behind the coffin, deeply moved to see that six hundred people had come to pay their last respects to the solicitor who believed law was to help people not to make the lawyers rich. He'd probably helped everyone present buy a house, make a will, sort out bereavement and probate or start a business. He wasn't much good on divorce. He'd light his pipe with St Bruno Ready Rubbed, and smoke the warring parties into a truce, then try to help them patch up their marriages. I'm convinced the thought of weeks of meetings with the smoke treatment kept many Pembrokeshire couples together. Most petty criminals were on first-name terms with my father. And hundreds of people in that church would still be waiting for the bills he'd forgotten to send from his shambles of an office.

It was only when he'd gone that I understood why he loved the place. A long way from the opportunities and certainties of city life, this was a town that could still call itself a community. Each mourner here would know everyone's name.

Under the bridge we sail, past Burton – the fairy tale Benton Castle hiding in the trees – around a bend in the Cresswell river and on to Lawrenny, famous in Tudor times for its oysters. We progress onwards up the Daucleddau. We used to motor up here in a little dinghy when we were kids. The cheap outboard engine would generally overheat at this stage and then we'd face the long row back to Pembroke Dock. My father said it was character-building, and he was right: I've made a point since of not buying clapped-out secondhand outboards.

At Llangwm we drop anchor. John, Paul, Will and I haul the punt over the side of *Mascotte* for the short journey to the shore. Thirty feet off the beach the punt's outboard motor breaks down, its propeller wrapped in thick, green weed. It is just like old times.

Ellen Skirm is in her 90s. Sitting on the bench looking across Llangwm beach, she remembers this village when it was a busy little port. Her grandmother was one of the original Llangwm women who still have legendary status in these parts: the Llangwm Cocklewomen. In her childhood, she says, the men of the village would fish and collect cockles and mussels, but it was the women who would trudge around the towns of Tenby, Haverfordwest, Pembroke Dock and Tenby selling their wares, gone for days at a time. The men, she said, would remain in the village or on the boats. The impression of feminist strength was further underlined by the women remaining known, albeit colloquially, by their maiden names, even after they married. I'd never thought of the banks of the upper Cleddau as an early stronghold of sisterdom. With a twinkle in her eye Ellen waves goodbye, delighted to see an ancient sailing boat moored off Llangwm once again.

Ellen Skirm

Further up river is Landshipping. At low tide soft mud holds numerous wooden boats, drying on the foreshore. Here the river divides into the Eastern and Western Cleddau. In the late afternoon sun this is a sight to behold: blue sky kissing dark green, ancient woods which meet the water's edge. All around us are remnants of a lost industrial age – stone jetties and decaying wooden pontoons. In the nineteenth century Landshipping was home to a large colliery, abandoned in 1845 after 42 miners were drowned when water broke into the workings.

Set back beyond high-water line, in amongst the trees, is a huge, centuries-old ruin of a once great house. This will one day be home to Alun Lewis and Sarah Hoss – they live in a couple of mobile homes behind their restoration project. But before I tap on their door, I wander around to see what they've let themselves in for. They are braver than me – this will take a lifetime of love and lots of money. Alan bounces out of their temporary accommodation with all the conviction of a man who knows there's no going back on his grand design. He runs diving and fishing trips. Sarah was a former colleague of mine in television, but she's given it up to come and live the good life on the banks of the Cleddau. Watching their children play in their huge garden on the side of the river, who wouldn't desert city life? Sarah offers to make dinner for us on the condition that we go and catch it.

Llangwm

Low tide at Landshipping

Alun and I wander over their garden to the wooden fishing boat his father and grandfather used. Watched intently by his spaniel – with its head cocked to one side – Alun pushes us off the mud and we spend an hour fishing with compass nets as generations of his family have done. Compass net fishing involves filtering the water passing beneath the boat with a large net. You hold the net frame with three fingers and when you feel a twitch you hope you've netted something edible. Catching dinner takes no more than half an hour – this is truly fast food.

On our return to the shore, the spaniel barks in anticipation of a good feast, while in the distance on the slipway a couple are arguing. The husband is reversing a cabin cruiser badly, then blaming his wife each time their trailer becomes stuck in the mud on the side of the concrete. Alun's children call this daily tourist performance 'the launch of the Birmingham Navy'. With absolutely perfect timing, just before a criminal act takes place, Alun's kids offer to tow the boat out of the mud with their tractor – for a token £20. This time next year they'll be millionaires.

We settle down to an early dinner in the garden looking onto the river; there follows a splendid feast of lobster, mackerel, beef and strawberries. I'd come here expecting to meet two weirdos who'd given up civilisation for roughing it – I leave without wanting to. These two have come to the upper Cleddau to restore a beautiful ruin and make a dream come true; even if their dream is never realised, it's a great place to watch and wait.

At six o'clock we take it in turns to be ferried in the dinghy to Alun's large motor boat, anchored in mid-channel. There's just half an hour in which to reach Haverfordwest at the top of the river on the high tide – something *Mascotte* couldn't do, but a boat with a shallow draught can just make it.

Alun and Sarah's restoration project
Compass net fishing

Haverfordwest, the county town in the middle of Pembrokeshire, started life as a crossing point of the river Cleddau. In its time it was a thriving port with coastal and foreign vessels sailing into the centre with cargoes of salt, iron, wine and apples. Exports from Haverfordwest included coal, slate, butter, oats, wheat, barley, hides and wool. But with the advent of larger vessels, the port fell into decline, and eventually the arrival of the railway brought an end to the town's waterborne trade.

Texaco oil refinery

We collect friends along the way to Haverfordwest, and a wonderful landscape passes by: small boats, Canada Geese, an ancient coal jetty, fishermen, rowers, tiny cottages and shocked campers nestled on the banks of the river. A heron ignores us as we turn the final corner below the castle, pass the old warehouses and tie up outside the Bristol Trader for a pint before the turn of the tide.

In the remains of the day, for us it's back on the punt to *Mascotte* and down the swollen Cleddau, with light failing and the sky purple, pink and blue. Beyond the bridge, Milford's tankers move slowly back and forth to their terminals or out to sea. Once again we pass Neyland, Scotch Bay, Gelliswick Bay, Sandy Haven, Great Castle Head, Watch House Point, and Monk Haven. At Dale, just before the mouth of the Haven, we drop anchor opposite Musselwick Point. Henry Tudor landed here in 1485 on his way to Bosworth Field where he defeated Richard to become King. Will and Simon hoist a light to the mast and, beneath a full moon, we open a bottle of Scotch for a nightcap.

Shipping Forecast

NORTH-EAST, THREE
OR FOUR, FIVE LATER

Return journey,
passing Llanstadwell

AT FIRST LIGHT, it's up the ladder to look out at the day. The Haven's tankers never sleep; already traffic is moving in and out of the terminals. It looks like another fine day for watersports at Dale, but we have a voyage to continue. We set off past St Ann's Head lighthouse, picking our way through lobster pots and by eight o'clock the sun burns my face. Even on a flat day, the Atlantic rushes the Irish Sea; the calmness of the water belies two fighting powers at work. The next headland on the navigation chart is called Vomit Point. This is a new one on me, but as the river Cleddau crashes into the Irish Sea one look at Helen, our radio producer, confirms this is well-named.

> 'The air of this county is said of strangers that resort thither from the inland parts of England to be very cold and piercing, but found to be very healthy to the county's inhabitants, seldom subject to infirmities, whereby the people live long and continue very perfect of health and memory.'

The Description of Pembrokeshire, George Owen

Dale

opposite page 'Mascotte in Solva'
by John Knapp-Fisher

Shipping Forecast

NORTHERLY WINDS 3 TO 4,
LOCALLY 5 IN WEST.
FAIR. GOOD VISIBILITY.

Within minutes the glassy sea turns into a frothing cauldron even on this hot summer's day. This is Jack Sound, where hundreds of ships have been claimed over centuries and in daylight you can see why. John Hart says the ocean is funnelled here into a narrow, shallow passage. Tony lines up clear of Skokholm conscious that at this state of the tide the high water conceals dangerous rocks. We play the navigation by the book and there's a happy ending.

Skokholm and Skomer pass by on the port side, dream destinations of another great journey we made a year ago; they look like old friends. At full sail

John Mapp-Fisher

2003

John Knapp-Fisher at Solva

we pass Anvil Point, Deadman's Bay and Wooltack Point, which marks the start of St Brides Bay and the wide stretch of sands of Newgale in the distance. There are no sun-worshippers yet, it's too early. Little Haven and Broad Haven will have a grand view of this beautiful ship under full sail. Druidston fort, now a hotel, stares out onto a clear blue sky and sea.

The Green Scar, Black Scar and The Mare rocks welcome mariners into our next port of call.

We anchor just off Solva and hoist the punt over the side. The inlet is full of small yachts and dinghies. At the slipway children with buckets of crabs meet us, and further up the beach, the artist John Knapp-Fisher is sketching in his notebook. He's painted this scene dozens of times: 'High water at Solva', 'Low water', 'Yachts on the sand', 'Boats on moorings', 'Blazing summer', 'Blue winter' – all framed and signed by John Knapp-Fisher. John draws in his pad sketches that he'll use as an *aide-memoire* while he works up a full painting back in his studio. There's no easel on location, no set of brushes, just a pencil and a book.

We adjourn to the The Harbour Inn for lunch. John lived on a boat for five years and sailed around Wales twenty-five years ago. He was shipwrecked off Aberystwyth. I ask him for his stories about his experiences in ports, expecting wise anecdotes about the challenge of painting a constantly moving scene, but instead he regales us with a tale of an evening in The Ship in Fishguard where he got so drunk he fell in the harbour.

After lunch John disappears in his three-wheeler, smoking his long pipe as he snakes through the village main street. He's promised to work up the drawings of *Mascotte* at anchor, our arrival by punt and Solva harbour. Knapp-Fisher is an old master and a work of art.

Solva Harbour

The tide has gone out and, at the slipway, the little shop selling dressed crab and lobster has sold all its food. We walk back along the dried-out sand to the water's edge. The beach revealed by low water is bustling with tourists, their rugs out and lunches spread over the tartan. Children, horses and dogs all play in the waves as we wade out to the waiting punt and head for *Mascotte*.

Inland a few miles from us is St David's Cathedral, hidden from the eyes of pirates and marauders on the sea.

The cross-currents of Ramsey Sound foam like a washing machine. Far off the port side The Bishops and Clerks rocks and then Point St John give way to Whitesands Bay and St David's Head. The names on the navigation chart change from English to Welsh as we move around the north Pembrokeshire coast. Despite the warm sunshine earlier in the day the weather now is less hospitable. The old pilot cutter rolls around Strumble Head and soon conditions at sea deteriorate to Force 5 – with the accompanying crash of crockery from the galley. A school of dolphins accompany us for miles, undeterred.

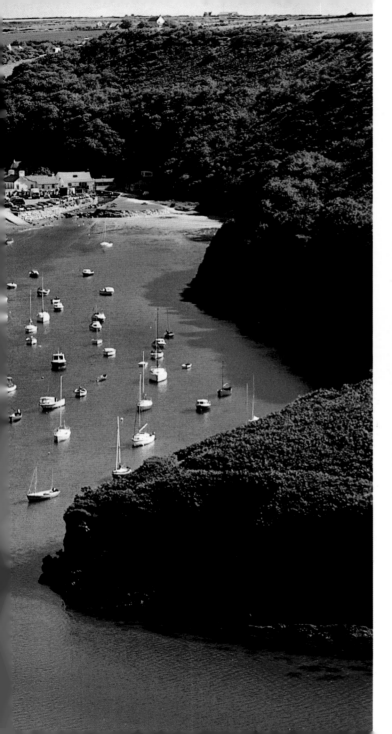

Fishing in Solva

Porthgain
Stormy weather

Past Monkey rocks, Abereiddi Bay, Porthgain, Trefin, Pwllcrochan and Aber Felin we keep a good pace. After some six hours, we make Fishguard and a wonderful sunset, a ball of fire falling into the water; then it quickly becomes cold.

The breakwater sticks out into Fishguard bay like an extended finger. Cameraman Jon Rees is leaving us for one day – he's off to a family wedding in Cardiff – so we move close to the jetty and he jumps into the darkness.

We move off the wall and drop anchor. It's John Hart's birthday and we crack open the champagne and dive into the cake, keen to snaffle it before the Irish ferry's bow wave throws us around. Unless you're a ferry passenger, visitors to Fishguard by sea are not well catered for. There's nowhere for a big old boat like this to tie up, no marina, though there is one planned. This stretch of the west Wales coast badly needs it.

Lower town, Fishguard
Fishguard to Rosslare ferry

07.00 Fishguard

Trying to go to the toilet or have a shower on a boat is none too easy, but when the ferry to Ireland is speeding past you, it becomes almost comical – thank goodness no one can see. Privacy is quite a scarce commodity on this boat.

The crew have all twigged that not only does Helen snore but she talks in her sleep. This could be very tricky over the coming days! The people who lived and worked on these boats must have got on very well, although it was an age when people generally didn't know much privacy on land.

Dinas Head, Ceibwr Bay and Cemaes slip by, and Poppit Sands scorch in the early sun. Dolphins provide a guard of honour as we sail past Cardigan Island. This is a stretch of coast I haven't sailed before; previously, I've headed north-west out to sea towards Bardsey. The Ceredigion coast is as beautiful as Pembrokeshire. I could happily step off the boat at any of these inlets and spend

Shipping Forecast

NORTH, TWO OR THREE

Strumble Head

New Quay

the day exploring, but we have people to meet and other places to see. Even though this will be the third time I've sailed around Wales, this journey simply tantalises with the hidden hamlets and villages I still don't know. It's as though another idyllic cliff-top smiles, keeping its secrets for another voyage.

For breakfast on deck Paul cooks bacon, sausage, eggs, beans, toast and hot coffee – a veritable feast. There are more dolphins and puffins on this stretch of sailing than anywhere else so far.

On the mainland just coming into view are the masts, radar and buildings of the military installation of Aberporth. Below, on the water small fishing boats at anchor are hopeful of a good day's catch, and the yellow sands of the town beach are already dotted with holiday makers.

John Hart stands on the foredeck and fixes a bearing on New Quay Head, as the beautiful bowl-shaped bay comes into view.

We're heading to Aberaeron and to enter it by sea is like coming in through

Heading for Aberaeron

the front door; it's like walking onto a film set, its splendid, coloured square houses offering an agreeable backdrop. I haven't got long here before the tide turns. Aberaeron is a long way from anywhere by land, and has been the victim of being located at the 'wrong end' of the supply chain.

Peter Bottoms is a fisherman. Rather than be finished off by fishing quotas, he takes sightseeing trips around the bay on his multi-purpose boat relaying the experience by webcam to his booking office on shore in order to entice the

Aberaeron harbour

Tony, Mags and John, plotting the course

Peter Bottoms, fisherman
Aberaeron harbour

undecided. Like most of waterside Wales, many of the houses in Aberaeron have been bought up by people who don't live in them. Properties here are now worth double their asking price five years ago – much to the delight of the people selling them and the dismay of youngsters who want to stay here.

Menna Heulyn is resplendent in her apron at the Harbourmaster hotel. She grew up here, went away and came back to open this boutique hotel in the middle of nowhere. Local people said she was mad. I've read about her in magazines just about everywhere, and the project is clearly a roaring success, with customers driving from miles around. It takes guts to take a huge gamble like this in a little harbour town but this has paid off handsomely.

Most of the harbour towns on this journey fall into two camps: the one mourning the heyday of times past when fishing or some other industry was king; and then those other communities whose people know that geography and economics are stacked against them, but rise to the challenge and reinvent

Menna Heulyn

themselves. Aberaeron is one of the latter. This has to be one of the most perfect looking harbours we sail to on this voyage and I'm truly sorry we leave after only a few hours – tide and time wait for no one, not even the BBC.

Some time after our sailing adventure I returned to Aberaeron as a guest at their Seafood Festival. My duties involved the onerous task of eating and drinking enormous amounts – the kind of engagement I'm keen to encourage. The harbourside was full of marquees selling seafood and local produce. Chefs from across the country braised, flambéd and fried, to the delight of onlookers. Lobsters were offered to eat cooked or raw, prawns pinked to perfection but too hot to handle for hungry spectators.

It's an interesting reflection on the way we live now that people in their hundreds come from far and wide to stand and stare in wonderment as chefs cook food. I guess we no longer cook or know how to cook or even see ingredients in their natural state. It was as though wizards were at work. I loved every moment.

ABERDYFI TO CAERNARFON

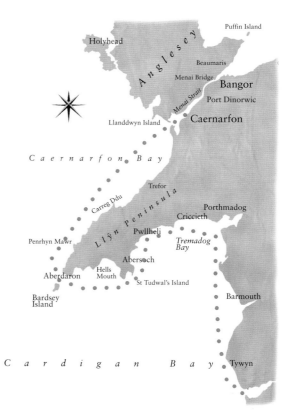

IN LATE AFTERNOON SUN the sails pause before filling, as if weary from August's heat. On the coast a huge television mast gives us a bearing with which to calculate our speed and time of arrival. Not that there's any hurry, but sailors do these things to while away the hours. The fire station tower marks out Aberystwyth in the distance, and the masts in its marina stick out like sticks on sausages. Our destination is further up the coast.

Aberdyfi is reached by navigating through its narrow channel over a notorious sandbar. Such is the reputation of John Hart and *Mascotte* that the harbour master comes out in his rib to meet us and guide us in. There is something wonderfully kind and considerate about the sailing fraternity; wherever we go we're met by so many people who help this lumbering old lady around Wales.

'When I cross the sea once more
Love comes knocking at my door
Like one, two, three, four, five and six
Of the bells of Aberdovey'

'The Bells of Aberdovey', from the opera
Liberty Hall by Dibdin

Shipping Forecast

THREE TO FOUR, FAIR,
OUTLOOK GOOD
'TIL WEDNESDAY

Oystercatchers at Aberdyfi

The Outward Bound barbecue

High tide at Aberdyfi

Students at Aberdyfi's Outward Bound Centre come from all over the world to spend a summer on the courses they run there – rock climbing, sailing, mountaineering, orienteering, camping and surviving in the great outdoors. I'm always interested in exploring perceptions of our country through the eyes of overseas visitors and readily accept an invitation to join in the centre's barbecue on the banks of the Dyfi estuary. Twenty or so students are our genial hosts by the side of a roaring camp fire on which they cook sausages and burgers, reward after an exhausting day in the great outdoors. This being an Outward Bound Centre, the copious amounts of hot dogs and relish can't be washed down with anything stronger than a drink of squash, much to the regret of the crew.

The students have been mesmerised by the beauty of this place – after three weeks in each other's company they have obviously become the best of friends and will be sorry to leave in a couple of days' time. Their summer in Wales, walking up Snowdon, sailing this estuary in gorgeous weather among new friends has made them good company and widened their horizons. After hearing what they love about Wales, I ask them about the less attractive aspects of Britain. A German lad of about fifteen, in perfect but accented English not unlike the German officer in

the television show *'Allo 'Allo* says, 'Vee don't like your sausages.' Probably a just criticism, coming from the country of the perfect banger. His comments bring the house down.

As we talk the evening away, the tide rises in the estuary beside us bringing a handful of canoeists following their instructor like colourful ducks. Most of the students on the Outward Bound course are teenagers from Italy, France, Germany, the Netherlands and some from Britain. At first, as is the case with so many people when television cameras are running, they were quiet and respectful, then soon they chatter away and are unstoppable. Politics, travel, music, their futures all come under discussion.

I can't help feeling inordinate sadness for one of them who later divulges that

Shipping Forecast

CALM, NORTH-EAST,
TWO

St Peter's church
The bells of Aberdyfi

she's there because her divorced parents couldn't agree what to do with her for the summer. They have been cared for wonderfully by the centre and made to feel part of a terrific, large family, but it is inescapable that a couple of them feel that on their return from a summer in Wales they will once again be an inconvenience to parents with new partners and new commitments.

After the barbecue we adjourn to Aberdyfi Sailing Club where advice for once again crossing the sandbar at the mouth of the estuary is freely offered. Cameraman Jon Rees returns from his family wedding in Cardiff – his toddler Ruby had stolen the show by removing all her clothes at the reception. By the time we wander out to find our ship, the water at the quayside has dropped sufficiently to make the 20-feet scramble down vertical ladders to *Mascotte*'s deck a daunting task even for the sober. Needless to say we sleep well.

Crabbing

09.00 Aberdyfi Quay

It's not every day that a hundred-year-old Bristol Channel Pilot Cutter sails into town and by the time we wake a sizeable crowd has assembled on the pier to wish us well. A lady who had been listening to my daily broadcasts for Radio Wales has followed us from Fishguard. Troubled by our cooker explosion, she has brought along a bottle of wine to keep us going. It's a most touching gesture and one I hope to encourage as we continue our journey.

St Peter's church clings to the seafront in Aberdyfi, its bells ringing out across the water. It's one of those places you can't simply pass – you have to go and explore. The churchyard is the town's history book, its inhabitants remembered in slate: David Thomas, infant son died 1850; Captain Humphrey Edwards, 1866; Jane Lewis beloved wife of Captain Elias Lewis departed 1862 aged 33; Sarah Anne beloved infant of J S Draper, Commander Indian Navy, aged 6 months. This is a walk back in time to a life that was hard and short for so many. Welsh folk legend has it that Aberdyfi is the nearest place on dry land to the hundred towns of the deep – a Welsh version of the lost city of Atlantis. The song 'The Bells of Aberdyfi' keeps the tale alive. The story goes that, at certain times, bells from beneath the waves can be heard.

I had great expectations of the church spire. The legend of the bells seemed to call for at least half a dozen bellringers, but when I round the last turn of the wooden staircase, it turns out to be rather like the scene from *The Wizard of Oz* when the curtain is pulled back on the Wizard. Malcolm is the lone campanologist

Planning our exit
Another couple of sea-dogs
The turnaround

and there are no ropes; he's pressing a large wooden keyboard and I try not to look disappointed.

By the time we are ready to leave Aberdyfi, the quayside is packed with families watching, children fishing off the pier, babies sleeping in their pushchairs and mums and dads waiting for something spectacular to happen. Fortunately for the spectators this is no ordinary departure. *Mascotte* is facing the wrong way for the off and has to be turned through 180° to face the right direction. With consummate skill Tony talks the crew through spinning this 50-ton boat with just ropes and the force of the tide. The crowd is delighted, their murmurs of approval punctuated by dogs on leads barking at the silent movement of something so large. Finally, a polite round of applause ripples through the crowd.

Through the channel crowded with dinghies, and the students from the Outward Bound Centre providing an escort, we set a course for Pwllheli. Beside us Cader Idris and Bird Rock look majestic in the early light. Before us across Tremadoc Bay the wide reach of the Llŷn Peninsula is like a swimmer's arm in the sea. Off to the starboard side lies Barmouth Bay and three hours' sailing before we cross St Patrick's Causeway.

Mascotte's escort

Mags listens to the shipping forecast because the weather conditions will determine our plans for our journey from here on. The Menai Strait ahead of us can only be entered in good conditions in such a large vessel.

'Of course, the BBC does sometimes get these forecasts wrong,' pipes up John Hart, who proceeds to recall the night when he was on the pilot boat off Barry when Michael Fish told the nation that a woman who rang the BBC to warn of an imminent storm had got it wrong.

On watch
The land crew

'One of the mates called me to look into the radar – there was an object coming towards us at 40 knots on the port bow. I turned the boat just in time to see a Butlins chalet pass us at sea. It was number 37 and the curtains were still closed!'

That man should be on the stage, but given how difficult the pilotage will be over the next few days, I'm glad he's here.

Our sails set for the day, we settle down to enjoy the sunshine. Will fastens a line off the stern to catch our tea, and we pass around the newspapers I bought in Aberdyfi early this morning. This is our first sight of the news for over a week, since there's no television or radio (other than VHF) on board. The headlines seem from a different world: America goes dark in electricity blackouts, a computer virus threatens worldwide chaos, Alastair Campbell prepares to go before the Hutton Inquiry. It's a long way from sailing an old boat across Tremadoc Bay.

There's little wind and we make slow progress, so we compensate with an early lunch of pasties from the Aberdyfi bakery, salad and fruit.

We haven't got much filming done today so Jon puts a waterproof splash bag on his camera and films Will's fishing line. In one of those moments that you could spend a life waiting for, a mackerel plays with the line and is eventually caught for supper and on camera – then another and another. In the end there are four splendid mackerel on line, so there'll be dinner at least for four of us.

Aberdyfi's channel buoy clangs in our gentle wash. By now there's barely enough wind to fly the red dragon which flutters limply on the mast. Straight ahead of us is Bardsey Island and closer, on the starboard bow, Pwllheli, where a yacht has all sails aloft but doesn't move. The dolphins have rejoined us, presumably after their lunch and play for the camera. John Hart curls up on the foresail lying on the deck; there's no better place for a snooze in the afternoon sun. In the far distance tiny, white triangles sail off the beach at Abersoch.

Within a few hours the wind picks up as the late afternoon temperature drops. A small fishing boat hurries home, a dozen yachts – red, white and cream – enjoy an evening sail and we make our way to Pwllheli with Snowdon beside us.

Richard Tudur's arrival out of the blue in a turbo-powered rib is an obvious clue that this guy travels everywhere very fast and doesn't like to be overtaken.

Approaching Pwllheli

That said, he's one of the most modest and unassuming people I've ever met. The round-the-world yachtsman whisks us off *Mascotte* and I can safely say I've never travelled so fast over water. I look down at his instrument panel just as I feel my teeth being forced out of the back of my neck: we're doing 40 knots.

Even viewed at speed, the sheer majesty of Tremadoc Bay with the mountains in the background is truly breathtaking. A tender takes us to the sailing club in Abersoch, where Richard is in the middle of organising a Sea Festival of sailing and watersports bringing in yachties from Ireland and across Britain. He's fiercely proud of the place and wants to make North Wales an international yachting

Sun-worshippers at Pwllheli

destination. It already looks pretty successful – the bay is full of dozens of yachts at anchor. In the late evening sunshine children play on the beach, stretching out the day before going home, and families gather round smoking barbecues on the sand. The doors to countless beach huts are open, revealing a young couple snogging in one, and elderly people hunched over a kettle in another. Richard says one of these huts recently changed hands for a fortune – living on the beach with a view like this, it must be worth it. We wander off to the pub in Abersoch for a pint before returning to Pwllheli by rib. *Mascotte*'s tied up to the fuel jetty but, helpfully, it's closed for the weekend! We're running short of fuel and water and plan to leave at 10 o'clock tonight for the Menai Strait.

Sunset, Pwllheli marina

Weatherman Derek Brockway sends me a text message warning of a deterioration in the weather; he's been helping us plan filming throughout this trip. It's been hot and sunny every day, so it would be a shame if it rained over the last few days. The ship's crew don't want to enter the Menai Strait or cross Caernarfon sandbar in poor weather conditions. Since we need ten feet of water beneath us, high winds and a heavy swell in the passage could ground us. So, to place us within spitting distance of the Strait, we leave for Llandwyn Island on an overnight sail.

There's a red moon tonight. I've only ever seen one in films so this is a treat. The stars are bright and Pwllheli lighthouse casts its beams over flat, cold water in bewitching sweeps. Sailing through the night brings out the confessional in all of us, as though in the absence of light we feel happy to discuss those things daylight precludes.

By the early hours, the lights at Pwllheli have receded and then disappear behind

us. In the darkness we sail over the oyster bank, past Abersoch and St Tudwal's Islands. Hell's Mouth Bay is disappointingly silent in the coldness of night.

The moon lights our passage through Bardsey Sound. I stayed on the island last summer and remember its people, cottages, lighthouse, hills and shores. It feels strange to be this close and to pass in the night without saying hello, but we have a timetable to get to the Menai Strait. Once again the time of high tide and the weather forecast set the pace.

We try to make out Porth Dinllaen, but the black coastline reveals nothing. If history had taken a slighty different turn Porth Dinllaen would now be a busy terminal and ferry port, but Holyhead was chosen instead. As far back as the 1830s, proposals were made to develop Porth Dinllaen as the main port linking Britain and Ireland; in the Archives Department of the university at Bangor you can read the 'Proposed London to Porth Dinllaen Railway Report'!

In the hour before dawn Paul makes breakfast and the smells of bacon, sausage and toast waft down the ship. We've anchored inside Caernarfon Bar on cue,

Tying up in Caernarfon

Shipping Forecast

EAST, TWO OR THREE

Castle and harbour, Caernarfon

though the skies have greyed and it's cold. This is the change of weather Derek promised. Under moody skies the mountains that last night appeared so romantic become threatening. A lone yacht moves quickly past the lighthouse near Llanddwyn Island pilots' cottages. A few feet beneath *Mascotte* lies the wreck of the *Grampian Castle*.

Suddenly during morning ablutions, a crisis – we've run out of water. I'm mid-lather in the shower when the dribble stops. Covering my modesty and with soap in one eye I deliver the news to my shipmates who receive it with varying degrees of sympathy. We change our plans and make for Caernarfon marina to fill the water tanks. We need fuel too, but this is Sunday in north Wales.

Feeding the swans

A further omen follows – cameraman Jon Rees's indestructible hat blows off into the water and floats away.

John Hart says when he was a pilot he would have to complete daily incident forms which he called 'whilst reports' to keep paper-loving civil servants happy. They were called 'whilst reports' because they would always begin, 'whilst proceeding . . .'!

So far, today's 'whilst report' is packed with incident. Whilst I am still drip-drying from my shower experience, Mags Hart helpfully says that on an ocean-going ship, two wet wipes count as a shower and six for a bath.

At midday we tie up in Caernarfon. The castle is spectacular from the sea and beneath it in the ancient port, the harbour master is wonderfully accommodating; gratefully, we fill up the old girl's water tanks.

With servicing done it's time to explore. Several small boys in tracksuits are fishing from the harbour walls. On the other side of the basin a large, new building is underway and I wonder if they'll cover this ancient harbour and its castle view with something grim like a supermarket. One new building is already occupied by the Caernarfon Record Office. Its pink walls are best forgotten, but the view from inside must be splendid. *Crackpot, Drifter* and *Wild Thyme* swing gently on their ropes below the timberyard full of sawn, yellow planks of Latvian pine. A fat labrador jumps in the water and takes its chances with the swans.

Then over coffee and cake at a cafe within the town walls, the talk is of Caernarfon's great potential as a yachting destination; it's so beautiful, and its port is right in the middle of the town.

On our return some viewers of the last television series we made about sailing around the islands of Wales are waiting on the pontoon with books to be signed. It's lovely to see them.

'A REGION OF MOUNTAINS, lakes, cataracts and groves in which Nature shows herself in her most grand and beautiful forms': George Borrow would be pleased to find that the description of Snowdonia in his book *Wild Wales* published in 1862 still holds good today. This is the land of Merlin, Arthur and his knights, Owain Glyndŵr and Llywelyn the Great. Arriving by sea here, you almost expect them to appear from the mountains.

The evening is spent anchored off the National Watersports Centre at Plas Menai, a couple of miles east of Caernarfon where we come upon generous hosts. In the last hours of daylight, beneath glowering skies, yachties clad in yellow are towed on their dinghies and windsurfers back to base, the youngest ones looking like ducklings. The centre is a marvel of sea training, and it's no wonder that students from all over the UK come here to learn or improve their competence on the water. It's a well-kept secret – I'm pretty certain few in the south and the west of Wales know of it – and yet there couldn't be a better place to learn about the sea. The Strait is one of the most demanding yet beautiful stretches of water Wales has to offer. We are given a guided tour around Plas Menai and then return on the rib to *Mascotte* off shore.

From the beach we can smell dinner! Paul's in the galley cooking

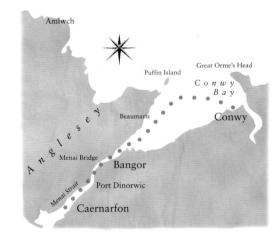

Mountain, bay and sandbank were bathed in sunshine; the water was perfectly calm; nothing was moving upon it, nor upon the shore, and I thought I had never beheld a more beautiful and tranquil scene.

Wild Wales, George Borrow

Learning the ropes
In training at Plas Menai

tagliatelli. Further up the shore a fisherman is standing up to his waist casting into the Strait. The tide has turned *Mascotte* at anchor since we left earlier.

After peaches and wine, Will hoists the lamp to the top of the mast, and there's time before bed for some more knot-tying classes with Mags. I'm hoping to gain my Competent Crew certificate on this voyage, which requires tying Bowline, Clove Hitch, Rolling Hitch, Round Turn and two half Hitches, Sheet Bend, Reef Knot and Figure of Eight. Director Sara Allen and radio producer Helen Callaghan are both faster than I am, simply from watching Mags teach me – it's very annoying.

Monday, Menai Strait

It's raining for the first time in ten days, no doubt an omen as I'm in charge of cooking breakfast. Lighting and cooking on a paraffin stove is an acquired skill that I have yet to acquire. On the menu: boiled eggs, tinned kippers, tomatoes, toast and tea. Catering for nine people would intimidate me in my own kitchen

Passing Plas Newydd

but in a small galley that is constantly moving in the wash of the water this is not an easy call. The paraffin stove is primed with meths on the burners which are then lit and allowed to burn out. The burners should at that point be sufficiently hot to switch on the paraffin. If, gentle reader, you can picture cooking whilst juggling with blowtorches you'll get the idea. To complicate matters, the microwave oven to cook the kippers is set behind the burners so that opening and closing its door requires dodging the moving pan of boiling eggs and the steaming kettle, all of which results in singeing the hairs on my arms. At least it overwhelms the smell of paraffin.

By midday, sunshine returns and tiny triangles of white leave the shore at Plas Menai for a day's sailing tuition. As we pull up the anchor white skies break up to show patches of blue.

On the river bank is Plas Newydd, home of the Marquess of Anglesey. Our

Shipping Forecast

WEST, FOUR

High and dry
Under Britannia Bridge

chatter on deck stops while we pass, admiring this beautiful house, largely remodelled in the eighteenth century by James Wyatt.

Kyffin Williams was waving one set of friends off when we arrived. His house is beside a small disused harbour, so he claims the title 'harbour master'. There are no ships here now, only ducks by the dozen – which he feeds. They look ridiculous waddling for dear life across the mud. The artist's home was once a pub called The Pilot Boat, but now, nestled in the tall trees, it looks as though it's been a painter's home for a hundred years. The view of the mountains, the Strait and the bridge is breathtaking, but Kyffin doesn't paint the view from

The artist Sir Kyffin Williams

here. His locations are further afield. He sketches on the mountains but retreats here to his studio to capture the outside world in magnificent oils. When I tell him about our voyage around the coast, he says he's only painted a few harbours and shows me his study of Holyhead.

We walk up stone steps to his studio, an old sailmaker's loft. There's a window in the roof (but not in the walls) protected by wire mesh and ensuring good light where Kyffin stands at his easel. Decades of paint tubes and old socks for wiping down, lie where they fell. On the table – his rainbow palette. The studio is packed to the rafters with canvasses to be sold at a show in London in May. Kyffin still paints two pictures a week, completing a large canvas in a single day. Most of the works in here are almost bigger than he is, so when he lifts huge pictures to the easel, he is all but overpowered by his art.

In the studio

I was here a year ago, and this time Kyffin is more at home, less defensive. Though he is rather more frail – even fragile – there is a passion and anger within him still. He fires a couple of broadsides against the modern art establishment. 'They don't know how to draw,' he says.

Outside, a handful of kids on the waterside throw stones at the ducks Kyffin fed earlier.

'Painting seascapes, harbours and boats is autobiographical,' he says handing down another canvas.

'What do your works say about you?' I ask him. He laughs and refuses to answer. He's from a generation that lets the work stand for itself, without quack psychological interpretation.

He shows me outside around the garden; high stone walls frame the lawn and a beautiful sculpture of a girl. More steps lead up to the top garden, where wild creepers hide his lookout towards the mainland.

We invite him back to *Mascotte* tied up at Menai Bridge. I expect him to decline the jetty and the leap of faith required to jump on deck, but he gamely comes along and has a cup of tea in the salon. Then he toddles off into the evening.

Night falls and a handful of teenagers arrive to fish off the jetty at Menai Bridge, ghetto blasters banging out garage music. It won't make for a quiet night but at least the fish will be grateful for the warning. Dinner on board tonight is vegetarian ravioli, potatoes, tinned asparagus, and rice pudding.

Three yachts tie up alongside us with the intention of tackling the Strait at first light, and their crews jump across our deck to catch last orders in the pub.

Telford's Menai Bridge

Lord Penrhyn
Bangor pier

Tuesday 08.00

The harbour master's labourer begins welding, bright and early, on the jetty wall. Skipper Tony almost has a fit when he sees sparks fly onto *Mascotte* – so we leave earlier than expected. Bacon-and-egg rolls and steaming coffee take the bite off a cold and grey morning that seems to have brought summer to an abrupt end.

Bangor pier, just a short hop away, has a large sign at its entrance: NO DOGS – and, sure enough, curled up only feet away is a large black cat, slumbering on the timbers, confident that dogs in Bangor can read.

Along the magnificent restored length of the pier, ice cream turret-like cones at regular intervals make homes for 'the fudge farm cabin', 'Bangor Civic Society', 'Andy and Wendy's handicraft' and 'Soroptimists'. None of them are in today, but it's clear the pier is where the action is here. There's another sign: 'Please don't put fish bait on seats.'

I wanted to go and explore Bangor cathedral but it's shut and I'm left

wondering why the Church in Wales thinks that God only works from nine to five.

Porth Penrhyn is our next destination. The castle and the Penrhyn estate were built on the profits of Welsh slate and Jamaican sugar. Today, the castle is owned by the National Trust and is a popular tourist attraction. In one of the bedchambers is a one-ton slate bed made for Queen Victoria – it sounds as uncomfortable as the bunk I'm sleeping in.

Scott Harman's boatyard in Porth Penrhyn looks like a little boy's bedroom floor, with toy-like boats in various states of disrepair standing around waiting for an ocean to sail. WOODEN BOAT BUILDERS AND REPAIRS. SHIPWRIGHTS, MASTS AND SPINNAKERS declares the sign above the workshop door. Outside, a dozen traditional wooden boats stand on stilts, like ducks out of water. The inside of the workshop is from another age, with its furnace in the corner being fed today with off-cuts from a keel, and the sweet smell of smoke from hardwood fills the air. Nailed to the wall are the nameboards *Tasma*, *Colchester*, *Gunna* and *Kelma* – all ships which have long gone.

The carcasses of *Elaine*, *Valerie* and *Enid* lie waiting attention, each one an expensive, high-maintenance and demanding mistress. To make good the sick joints of these ageing old ladies, the craftsman will select what he needs from a hundred boxes containing bronze fittings, screws and eyelets. They are all stacked

Scott Harman's workshop
Porth Penrhyn

In need of tender loving care
Casting off

Shipping Forecast

WEST, THREE OR FOUR,
FIVE LATER

in racks above the benches, as in an old chemist's shop. The handtools scattered across the benches were made in another century and have outlasted generations of craftsmen who sawed, planed and chipped. On the floor there's sawdust of mahogany, ash, oak and iroko.

This morning *Espanola*, built in 1903 for the King of Spain, looks humbled – her decks removed, floor timbers under repair, oakum and red-lead putty caulking the cavities of toothy planks. Her return to grace will mean copper sheathing for her hull, new beam shelves, horn timber, new counter and mast, and a coating of the black paint Samuel Bond of Birkenhead used when he built her a century ago.

We make our way back to our century-old boat in the Strait outside the harbour. At low tide three friends stand netting on the sand at the water's edge. The mountains are stubbornly shrouded in cloud today, though a weak sun tries in vain to warm the dark green canvas of fields. I'd thought Kyffin's paintings of this area could sometimes be gloomy but today they'd look like a photograph. These are his mountains.

On the opposite shore Beaumaris's small square houses in orange, pink, yellow and blue look like liquorice allsorts scattered along the shoreline, their black roofs sparkling in occasional sunshine. The town pier is full of children endlessly fascinated by the seagulls, fish and water below. Dozens of generations must have stood here looking out to Puffin Island, watching the tide come in and out; it's the best show in town. From here Bangor across the water looks like the backcloth of a school musical production, with three distinct layers to the set – water, houses and outsize mountains behind.

The end of the Menai Strait is a narrow channel at low tide. Only yards away from us, yachts stand still in the sand, left high and dry. This is Conwy Bay, past

Penmaenmawr

Heading for Conwy

Last port of call, overlooking Deganwy

Puffin Island, past the lighthouse with its black and white circular bands, and 'No passage landward' written large on its stone. Its bell clangs like a demented clock in the rising breeze. *Gale Force*, a red dinghy the size of a pocket handkerchief, crowded with four fishermen, struggles to pass us as it's thrown around on the wash. A larger, open boat carries divers spending the day exchanging the grey sky for the grey deep.

Once we're in open water there's more tuition for my Competent Crew examination; more knots with Mags. John Hart tells a story of navigating in thick fog before the days of GPS. He used a depth sounder, he explains. 'This may not tell you where you are, but it will tell you where you are not,' he says. So I add this to my list of knots.

The crew have decided that discipline has broken down on board, largely due to the influence of these louche television types, and that we should revert to a more formal nomenclature. Henceforth Tony will be known as Mr Winter, John as Mr Hart, the boys Will and Paul both Master Winter. This plan hits trouble when it's pointed out that Mags will be Madam Hart . . .

In Conwy Bay I take my turn at the helm. There are few experiences quite so wonderful as steering this boat, all sails aloft, with no sound except wind and water. It's a timeless feeling and I'll miss these moments when the voyage comes to an end tomorrow.

Conwy's harbour master meets us in his launch at sea. Guiding our vessel into the tight confines of his manor and all its acres of expensive glass fibre yachts will

Will, climbing the mast
Conwy castle

The night watch, Conwy

not be easy. Our first task is to refuel. The fuel jetty, built for yachts of half the size and a tenth of the weight, looks like flimsy matchboard as Tony brings her in. To someone of less experience, coming alongside here in *Mascotte* seems like parking a bus on a penny.

The harbour master guides us through the channel to our berth in the shadow of Conwy Castle. Beneath its walls are a throng of people, and a sightseeing boat unloads dozens more camera-laden tourists holding their hands to their eyes to shield them from the afternoon sun. A middle-aged couple pass us in a hired dinghy ignoring each other. The Liverpool Arms lies an enticing row away from our pontoon off the shore. Beside us the dinghies *Rest a While, Serendipity, Jeanette* and *Galloway* flash back sunlight across the water.

The final chapter

On the shoreline a small sailing boat, a 1924 Welsh knobby named *What O*, is for sale in its original state – a lifetime of adventures for the price of a small car. The shingle is covered with plastic dinghies upturned like turtles waiting for the high tide. An impossibly large woman tries to squeeze into the front door of THE SMALLEST HOUSE IN BRITAIN. I'll wait 'til she leaves before entering.

Paul and Christine Gibbs's Teapot Museum is a short walk from the water. Only in Britain would we have a sanctuary for tea. The celebrated Worcester teapot of 1880, Thomas Whieldon-Wedgwood's cauliflower pot *circa* 1775 and the wigwam pot designed by Clarice Cliff in 1930 are in august company among thousands of other pieces. (I was dying for a cuppa but didn't think it was the place to ask.)

In the early evening, the land crew following us with another camera on the coast send a text to say they're in a pub quiz in Conwy and ask for help with questions. We try hard, but despite the BBC's unseen team being twice the size of the other competitiors, we only manage second place. Dismayed, the runners-up come aboard later for a final nightcap – and *Mascotte*'s crew present me with my Competent Crew (traditional boat) Certificate. I look carefully to check they haven't doctored it with 'incompetent'.

There's a curious feeling on our boat. Skipper Tony Winter, his son Will and pilot John Hart begin planning *Mascotte*'s return voyage to Cardiff. Gales are expected but they may avoid the worst by sailing straight to the Irish coast from north Wales. There are new navigation charts out on the table below, plans for a different voyage. Mags is making mobile phone calls to the sailing students she will teach in Barry on Monday; John gets a call from the crew of a yacht he's to deliver across the Atlantic next week. This is where we part company after our summer's sail around the harbours of Wales one sunny August. Everyone feels a curious mix of weariness after this mad dash and yet regret that it's at an end. Cameraman Jon Rees sees a Chinese toddler with her parents on the quayside and I know he's missing his little girl. I'm tempted to buy all the newspapers, like a good hack should, to catch up on all I've missed, then I hestitate. Not just yet. We've spent the last two weeks watching the world from a distance, outside observers looking on and quietly leaving at dawn. We've completed nearly three hundred miles of sailing in a hundred-year-old boat, with nineteen ports of call. This is the end of our adventure.

The mutinous crew

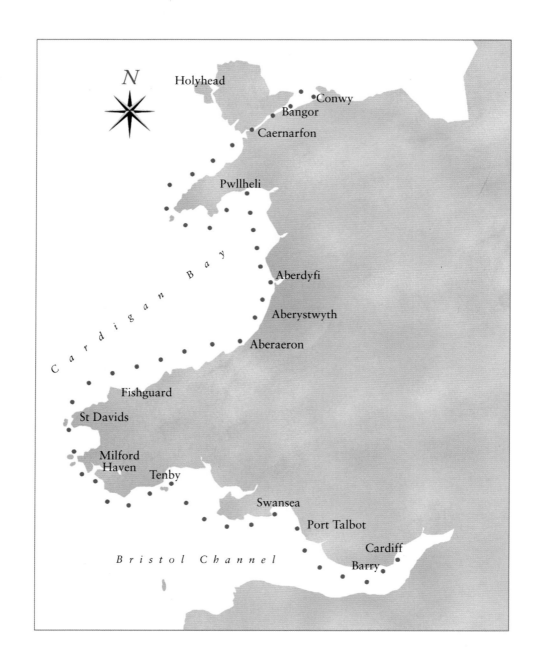